TRUMPET

SMOOTH JAZZ

TITLE	PAGE	TRACK WITH MELODY CUE	TRACK ACCOMPANIMENT ONLY
Morning Dance	3	1	2
Bali Run	4	3	4
Just the Two of Us	6	5	6
This Masquerade	8	7	8
Silhouette	9	9	10
Harlem Nocturne	10	11	12
Songbird	12	13	14
Breezin'	13	15	16
Tourist in Paradise	14	17	18
She Could Be Mine	16	19	20
We're in this Love Together	18	21	22

ISBN 978-0-634-02769-7

HAL•LEONARD®
CORPORATION

7777 W. BLUEMOUND RD. P.O. BOX 13819 MILWAUKEE, WI 53213

Visit Hal Leonard Online at
www.halleonard.com

MORNING DANCE

By JAY BECKENSTEIN

1: With melody cue
2: Accompaniment only

TRUMPET

BALI RUN

By LEE RITENOUR
and BOB JAMES

TRUMPET

5

JUST THE TWO OF US

CD

5: With melody cue
6: Accompaniment only

TRUMPET

Words and Music by RALPH MacDONALD,
WILLIAM SALTER and BILL WITHERS

with Synth. solo

Keyboard break

4

mf

f

mf

THIS MASQUERADE

CD

Words and Music by
LEON RUSSELL

TRUMPET

SILHOUETTE

By KENNY G

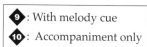

HARLEM NOCTURNE

Music by EARLE HAGEN

CD

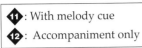

11: With melody cue
12: Accompaniment only

TRUMPET

11

SONGBIRD

CD

⬥**13** : With melody cue
⬥**14** : Accompaniment only

By KENNY G

TRUMPET

BREEZIN'

Words and Music by
BOBBY WOMACK

TRUMPET

TOURIST IN PARADISE

By RUSS FREEMAN

TRUMPET

Jazz Rock
Keyboards

SHE COULD BE MINE

By DON GRUSIN

CD

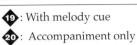

19: With melody cue
20: Accompaniment only

TRUMPET

WE'RE IN THIS LOVE TOGETHER

CD
21: With melody cue
22: Accompaniment only

Words and Music by KEITH STEGALL
and ROGER MURRAH

TRUMPET

rit.